Mastering Your Pre-Screen Recording
A Comprehensive Guide to Succeeding in Your Path to
Universities, Competitions, and Professional Careers in the Performing Arts

By Diego Barbosa-Vásquez

A Publication of
Performing Arts Laboratory - Press

Mastering Your Pre-Screen Recording
A Comprehensive Guide to Succeeding in Your Path to
Universities, Competitions, and Professional Careers in the Performing Arts

By Diego Barbosa-Vásquez
Opera, Orchestra, and Ballet Conductor & Scholar
Doctor in Music & Expert in Performing Arts Sustainability
www.barbosavasquez.com

Printed Paperback - First Edition: Nov 2024
ISBN: 979-8-9917108-0-0

Performing Arts Laboratory - Press
Bloomington, IN, USA
www.PerformingArtsLab.com

Table of Contents

About

Mastering Your Pre-Screen Recording

A Comprehensive Guide to Succeeding in Your Path to
Universities, Competitions, and Professional Careers in the Performing Arts
By Diego Barbosa-Vásquez

Drawing from over a decade of groundbreaking and internationally awarded practical-research, this publication distills the latest insights on creating outstanding Pre-Screen recordings for university applications, competitions, and professional opportunities. This guide is part of the Performing Arts Laboratory - Press, a branch dedicated to transforming complex, multidisciplinary research into accessible, practical resources for the performing arts community. Available in multiple languages, Performing Arts Laboratory - Press publications ensure that everyone, regardless of background or level of expertise, has the tools to engage with the performing arts and, for artists or arts administrators, to enjoy a sustainable and fulfilling career in the field.

Published by: Performing Arts Laboratory - Press

Diego Barbosa-Vásquez

Opera, Orchestra, and Ballet Conductor & Scholar
Doctor in Music & Expert in Performing Arts Sustainability

Maestro Diego Barbosa-Vásquez is a Colombian-born Opera, Orchestra, and Ballet Conductor & Scholar. Worldwide trained and currently based in the USA. He is the General Director of the Performing Arts Laboratory (USA) and Music Director of The Americas Chamber Orchestra. Maestro Diego is recognized as a "Musical Genius" by the international press and is Official Ambassador of Colombia (Country Brand) since 2017. He has gained international recognition through his performances across the globe, by representing Latin America in conducting competitions, conferences, and events, and is recognized for his major scholarly/practical contributions to the Performing Arts field.

Maestro Barbosa-Vásquez has collaborated as Conductor with the St. Louis Symphony Orchestra, Indianapolis Symphony Orchestra, Nashville Symphony Orchestra, Cincinnati Symphony Orchestra, IU Opera and Ballet Theater, and IU Symphonies (USA). In addition, was Music & Artistic Director of the CASC Opera Camp and the World Music

Symphony Orchestra (Los Angeles, CA); Music & Artistic Director of Pronartes Musical Theater, Huila Philharmonic, and E&P Orchestra and Choir System (Colombia), and Principal Guest Conductor of El Salvador National Youth Symphony Orchestra for 6 years, between other Artistic Director positions at USA and Latin America.

Moreover, the Colombian Maestro holds a Doctor Degree from the prestigious Opera, Orchestra, and Ballet Conducting Department at Jacobs School of Music of Indiana University (USA) with Doctoral Minors in Music Theory and Arts Administration. A Master's Degree in Opera and Orchestra Conducting from Azusa Pacific University, a double Bachelor Degree in Opera, Orchestra, and Choral Conducting and in Viola, with Minor in Chamber Music from Juan N. Corpas University (Colombia), and an Associate degree in Orchestra Administration from the Global Leaders Institute of the Orchestra of Americas.

Furthermore, Maestro Barbosa-Vásquez is a Multidisciplinary Scholar internationally recognized for his PostDoctoral Research in LatinAmerican Cultures, Arts and Identities collaborating with centers as CLACS (Center of Latin American and Caribbean Studies) as Artists/Scholar, and for his PostDoctoral Research in Performing Arts Sustainability (Dimensions: Artistic, Financial, Social and Ecological) with emphasis on International Business, International

Political-Economy, Entrepreneurship, and Public Policy development collaborating with the prestigious Ostrom Workshop USA (winners of Economic Nobel Prize) as affiliated scholar.

For more information about Maestro Diego Barbosa-Vásquez, see his full Biography, see his videos, read his academic production, or know more about his future concerts and scholar activities, scan this QR code or visit this website

www.barbosavasquez.com

Performing Arts Laboratory

Based on in-depth international practical research and award-winning multidisciplinary work, the Performing Arts Laboratory (PAL) develop sustainable and profitable productions, comprehensive services for organizations and individuals, advanced products and courses, and state-of-the-art resources in easily digestible formats. All of these efforts are designed to serve and enhance the Performing Arts field (Opera, Orchestra, and Ballet). Through a multidisciplinary approach—collaborating with fields such as economics, business, arts, anthropology, social sciences, arts administration, political economy, macro and microeconomics, and entrepreneurship— PAL assist organizations, artists, and societies at local, regional, national, and international levels in understanding and leveraging the keys to achieving sustainability in the performing arts.

Every stakeholder in the performing arts is crucial. The Performing Arts Laboratory (PAL) support artists and arts administrators in building stronger and healthier careers, help organizations adopt more sustainable artistic practices, business structures, and services, and serve communities, whether local or global, to benefit from increased collaboration and engagement within the Performing Arts experiences. Ultimately, PAL aim to develop solutions that contribute to a more sustainable Performing Arts field benefiting the full spectrum of stakeholders involved.

For more information about the
Performing Arts Laboratory,
scan this QR code or visit this website

www.PerformingArtsLab.com

Barbosa-Vasquez Private-Studio

Barbosa-Vásquez/Private-Studio is an online space for talented individuals from around the world who seek rigorous training in a challenging environment with an international perspective on musical excellence and artistic development. With a carefully designed, personalized curriculum and close weekly guidance from Maestro Barbosa-Vásquez, each student works hard to build a significant career in music, regardless of their major or location.

The studio offers four certified programs (valid in USA, Colombia, and Türkiye), each fully tailored to achieve the best possible results for every student. With close attention from an international faculty and direct mentorship from Maestro Barbosa-Vásquez, all programs grant certifications valid in all three countries, and access to state of the art training for multiple levels (professionals, mid levels, and beginners).

The studio primarily focuses on online sessions, allowing students to maintain regular, weekly lessons regardless of where they live or where Maestro Barbosa-Vásquez is conducting. This approach accommodates Maestro's international responsibilities while offering students the flexibility to manage their own time and commitments more effectively. Additionally, students are welcome to attend in-person classes at Maestro Barbosa-Vásquez's studios in Los Angeles (CA) and Bloomington (IN) in the USA, Bogotá in Colombia, and Bursa and Bodrum in Türkiye, depending on his yearly schedule.

To be part of this Private-Studio, study directly with Maestro Barbosa-Vásquez
or get special coachings for pre-screen and auditions, scan this QR code or visit this website

www.barbosavasquez.com/studio

Prologue

Hi there! If you are a performer preparing your Pre-Screen materials, this guide was specially designed for you. In this comprehensive guide, we will cover all the knowledge you need to create outstanding Pre-Screen recordings for your applications to universities, competitions, and professional positions.

As a winner of multiple international scholarships and grants at the undergraduate, master's, doctoral, and postdoctoral levels; having been invited to represent my country and continent in prestigious competitions; and winning many professional positions in various countries, I will share with you all the basics of a successful Pre-Screen recording. Additionally, from my experience on the other side as a jury member for many Pre-Screen auditions at different levels, and as a principal investigator developing groundbreaking practical research on Performing Arts Sustainability, I will provide you with advanced insights and 21 Pro-Tips. With this publication, we aim to ensure that you not only have the best Pre-Screen recording experience but also set yourself up to receive invitations for in-person auditions and the positions you're aiming for.

This is a good moment to make an important clarification. This publication is intended for individuals who already possess the technical, musical, and artistic skills needed to record Pre-Screen materials. It is not a "learn how to play, dance, act, or sing" type of guide. There are several reasons for this, but the most important one is that learning how to play, sing, act, or dance is an art in itself. It requires not only time but also proper professional and personalized guidance, which a book cannot provide. Therefore, if you are looking to learn how to play, sing, act, or dance, I recommend seeking a local mentor or program in your area, or you can explore Barbosa-Vásquez Private Studio, an international studio (referenced earlier in this publication). These are the places dedicated to this type of work, which is crucial before considering a Pre-Screen recording.

I want to extend my gratitude to Performing Arts Laboratory-Press, Intersociedad-E&P Foundation, and Barbosa-Vásquez/Private-Studio sponsors. Their unconditional support has made this publication possible. We all share the firm mission of ensuring that every Performing Artist, regardless of their level, country, or financial situation, has access to the best possible resources for their profession. We are committed to helping artists continue growing in their artistic paths and shaping the world into a better, more artistic place.

Special thanks also go to all my mentors, colleagues, and friends in the Performing Arts field who played a crucial role in the development of groundbreaking practical research on Performing Arts Sustainability.

And of course, thank you to my wife Deniz, my brother Juan Sebastian, and my mother Leonor. You are always an inspiration, and your unconditional support has been invaluable at every step of my career.

Therefore with no more things to say here, let's start!

Chapter 1: Repertoire Preparation

What is Pre-Screen Material

To begin this guide, it's essential to clarify what Pre-screen Materials are and why they play a crucial role for anyone pursuing a career in the performing arts.

Along with your CV, Pre-screen materials serve as the first filter that performing arts programs or organizations use to select a smaller number of candidates from a large applicant pool for in-person auditions. For the most exclusive programs or organizations, this process ensures that only the top-tier applicants are invited to audition. In contrast, for less competitive programs, pre-screen materials help ensure that selected performers meet the minimum required skill levels.

Pre-screen materials typically consist of a series of recordings of specific repertoire, monologues, choreographies, or other performances, depending on the applicant's major and desired position. Each program or organization tailors its pre-screen requirements based on the type of artist they seek, their upcoming performance repertoire, the faculty's expertise, and other factors. In short, pre-screen materials are a performer's formal first impression before a panel of judges, allowing them to determine whether the applicant is a good fit for the program or organization.

You can find more in-depth information about all the logics behind the Pre-Screen Materials and why programs and organizations required them on my Doctoral Dissertation.

You can access it for free on my website or by scanning this QR code.

Just like any first impression, it can last only a few seconds if not done well, or it could mark the beginning of a long-term professional relationship that shapes your career. Therefore, it's crucial to approach this stage with care and proper preparation as it can close or open multiple doors in your career.

There are multiple steps that must be followed to create outstanding Pre-screen materials, and in the following chapters, we will describe all of them. However, the most important step is understanding that from this point forward, regardless of your level, you are an artist, and your pre-screen material must reflect that. If you can showcase your artistry in your pre-screen, a significant part of the pre-screen challenge has been accomplished.

Defining the Repertoire

Now, moving into action, everything that becomes successful starts with proper planning! Before diving into any practice or recording, the first step in creating your Pre-Screen materials is to carefully review the repertoire requirements for each university, competition, or position you're applying for. Many schools, competitions, and professional programs have specific guidelines for their Pre-Screen auditions. It's essential to understand these requirements in detail before you begin preparing.

Create a comprehensive list of all the requested repertoire across the different auditions you're considering. This will help you identify overlapping pieces that you can reuse and determine which ones suit your current level and which ones might require additional preparation. This approach will save both time and effort.

<u>Focus on quality over quantity.</u> Pre-Screen recordings should showcase your absolute best playing, acting, singing, dancing, or conducting. It's wise to stick to a small selection of repertoire that you can polish to the highest standard, rather than spreading your energy too thin.

<u>Important note:</u> Since conductors are often required to present Pre-Screen materials that involve conducting an orchestra, some of the steps described here may not fully align with their specific needs. If you need extra help or guidance, feel free to contact me directly through my website. However, despite these differences, the underlying logic of preparing Pre-Screen materials is very similar for both performers and conductors. Therefore, this guide is still worth reading.

Understanding Contrasting Repertoire

One common requirement in auditions is to present contrasting repertoire. But what does "contrasting" actually mean?

At its most basic level (usually for undergraduate entry), it simply refers to pieces that convey contrasting moods, such as:

- Happy vs. Sad pieces
- Fast vs. Slow tempos
- Dramatic vs. Joyful moods

- Long notes vs. Short notes
- Etc.

As you move beyond the basics, especially at the Master's degree level, "contrasting repertoire" still refers to contrasting moods, but also involves contrasting styles. This means your Pre-Screen should demonstrate a wide range of understanding across different styles and eras.

  - **Baroque, Classical, Romantic, Modern, and Contemporary** music each demand distinct instrumental techniques, artistic sensibilities, and interpretive choices. Demonstrating the ability to navigate these styles with authenticity is essential to showcasing your versatility.

Now, at the Doctoral and Professional levels, "contrasting" becomes much more specific. It not only includes the mood and basic stylistic understanding mentioned earlier but also requires a deep comprehension of each composer's full body of work and how it relates to performance, whether in "historical performance" (replicating the sounds of the time when the pieces were composed) or in more standard performance practices.

  - For example, when preparing a classical piece, it's not enough to simply **distinguish between**

Haydn, Mozart, or Rossini. You must go further, understanding early vs. late Haydn, or how classical performance practices in Rossini have evolved from the 1980s to today.

- **Consider how technique changes.** For instance spiccato differs in a Mozart work compared to a Rossini or Haydn composition, and how the overall musical arc is distinct and "contrasting."

Understand, differentiate, and recognize the "contrasting" elements within the same piece.

Going even further, for example in *Falstaff*, an outstanding opera that encapsulates various compositional styles and eras of opera, many characters evolve throughout the performance. This requires a much deeper understanding of their full artistic and technical development.

Of course, "contrasting repertoire" at the professional level involves performance practices analysis, which is a very in-depth subject. Since this is not the primary focus of this publication, I'll direct you to another article where you can explore this topic in greater detail: *The Art and Science of Performance: Unlocking Mentor-Mentee Tradition in the Arts.* You can access it for free on my website by scanning the following QR Code:

<u>Important note:</u> Please don't feel overwhelmed by these more specific "contrasting" requirements if you're not yet at this level. If the topics I'm describing here seem difficult or feel like I'm speaking another language, don't worry. A good Pre-Screen recording depends on your specific level. As I've outlined the levels of "contrasting" repertoire required at different stages, just focus on where you are right now and go for it! With more experience, you'll naturally progress to more demanding elements in time. Trust the process.

PRO TIP 1: Standard Performance Practices

For master or undergraduate programs, always aim for "standard" performance practices in your recordings. The goal is to show the jury that you have a solid grasp of the accepted norms for interpreting a piece. Use reliable, standard editions of scores that are widely recognized and avoid those that may add unconventional markings or instructions. For auditions, juries typically seek performers who can confidently deliver a recognized interpretation without straying too far into personal or avant-garde choices.

PRO TIP 2: Tailoring Your Repertoire and Performance Approach to the Specific Program or Organization

Your repertoire choices should reflect the specific nature of the program or professional role you're applying for. For instance, if you're applying to a historical performance practice program at the PhD level, your concept of "contrasting repertoire" will be very different from that of someone applying for a position with a modern symphony orchestra, and your Pre-Screen materials must reflect that.

For example, if you're auditioning for a prestigious orchestra like the Vienna Philharmonic versus the Berlin Philharmonic, Concertgebouw Orchestra, New York Philharmonic, or the Los Angeles Philharmonic (just to name a few), you'll want to demonstrate that you understand the unique sound and stylistic approach of each orchestra. Different orchestras, opera companies, and musical theater organizations have distinct interpretations of how the repertoire should be performed and how composers should be approached, and demonstrating your understanding of those nuances can set you apart at this competitive level.

Similarly, at the undergraduate and master's levels, a quick review of the current and past repertoire, as well as videos of the university orchestra, opera studio, and musical theater productions, can give you a good sense of the type of profile they are looking for in their current and future students.

What to show in the recording

The main purpose of the Pre-Screen recording requirement is to serve as the first filter to select a small number of candidates from a large pool of applicants. Every program, competition, or organization is different, and their acceptance rates vary; however, for the most prestigious ones, the rate of people called to in-person audition is around 5% to 10%. What this means is that the combination of your CV and your Pre-Screen materials has a 90% chance of resulting in rejection.

More information about these percentages can be found in my Doctoral Dissertation "Models for the Creation and Leadership of Sustainable Opera Camps". You can access it for free on my website or by scanning this QR code.

Mastering Your Pre-Screen Recording

In general, the higher the level of the program or organization you are applying to, the more complex it is to secure an in-person audition. From the jury's perspective, it becomes increasingly difficult to determine which candidates should be invited for the limited spots in the in-person auditions. Therefore, the selection is based on a very selective combination of the Pre-Screen materials and the CV.

Don't get discouraged; many of the 90% who are rejected make mistakes in their Pre-Screen materials. The fact that you are reading this guide will significantly increase your chances of being invited to an in-person audition.

Creating a CV is "an art" in itself and is a topic separate from what we are addressing in this publication. As we are partnering with the Performing Arts Laboratory for this publication, I will refer you to them and their amazing course designed for individuals like you. There, you can learn how to create a standout CV tailored for your dream job or school in the Performing Arts! The course will guide you step-by-step on how to craft a unique and impactful CV that highlights your strengths and aligns with the specific needs of the arts field. Just visit the Performing Arts Laboratory website (www.PerformingArtsLab.com) and look for courses. Or simply scan this QR code to access it

You can use the code "Pre-Screen/Guide2024" for a 20% discount on the CV course if you are interested in their assistance.

Returning to the Pre-Screen, which is the focus of this publication: because of the highly competitive environment you are entering, the jury wants to ensure that you possess the basic technical mastery and artistic depth required for the program or organization. The way to evaluate this (at least from the Pre-Screen perspective) is by analyzing how you approach each repertoire piece in two key areas: Technical Skills and Artistic and Interpretive Knowledge.

- **The technical skills** include accurate intonation, rhythmic precision, good sound production, articulation, acting skills, and diction (for singers), as well as the ability to navigate difficult passages with ease at your specific level.

Note for conductors: The technical criteria are much more demanding in this context, as conducting technique is highly personal. However, there are specific elements that juries evaluate in your pre-screen in this area. To explain them thoroughly would require a lot of text. Therefore, if you are interested in that aspect, and to avoid creating a 30-page description that would be only useful for conductors, I invite you to review the second chapter of my Doctoral Dissertation, specifically the section on conducting (I shared the link few pages above). It will clarify many aspects for you. Now, if you still have questions or need help, do not hesitate to reach out directly at my website: www.barbosavasquez.com.

- **Artistic and interpretive knowledge** involves presenting a thoughtful, informed interpretation of the music that goes beyond simply playing the right notes. Having something unique to say about the music can make your performance stand out. Naturally, the more experience and higher level you have, the deeper this conversation can go, so always strive to do your best in this area.

PRO TIP 3: You are an artist SHARE A MESSAGE!

No matter your level, whether beginner or advanced, every time you play, YOU ARE AN ARTIST. Remember that, in the end, all we do is to SHARE A MESSAGE or broadcast a value. Therefore, ensure that your Pre-Screen has something interesting to say (for both you and the listener) about the piece. Learn about the work from a historical and theoretical perspective (at your level), analyze how it connects to you, reflect on it, and discuss it out loud with yourself or a friend. When playing, take time to reflect on it in your mind (there's no need to say it aloud in the recording). Remember, this is why you are in this field: to SHARE A MESSAGE. Believe me, juries can sense that too.

Selecting the pieces to record

With all the information above, you now have a better understanding of the kind of repertoire you will need to record. Now is the time to move on to specific pieces, excerpts, etc. To do that, there are some straightforward steps to follow:

1.   Review (yes, once again) very carefully what repertoire each university or organization is asking for in each application. If you are applying to more than two, it is very common to misplace information.

Depending on the level, this will give you either a clear list of specific pieces or a broad range.

2.   For specific requests, simply record the exact piece and excerpts they ask for; do not send any others! Many programs do not commonly provide such specific guidelines. Therefore, if they do, there are important reasons for it, and sending something outside of that will likely result in immediate rejection. If you cannot send the specific materials they are requesting, for your own strategic time management reasons, it's better to either contact them to ask for flexibility or to skip submitting your application entirely.

3.   The complexity arises with Pre-Screen requirements that are more flexible (e.g., send a Classical concerto, a Romantic sonata, or a Bach sonata; or select a monologue or an aria, etc.). Selecting the specific pieces is an art by itself because every person is totally different. Here is where you need to be very strategic and some pro-tips are helpful.

PRO TIP 4: Record something you already performed.

If possible, try to record something you have already worked on. Yes, sometimes using recording opportunities is a great way to increase your repertoire, but a Pre-Screen is not the best moment for that. If there is something you have already performed that works for the Pre-Screen, this is the way to go; the results will always be much better that way.

PRO TIP 5: Always select repertoire that makes you shine!

If you excel at low notes, choose repertoire that exploits that strength. If your vibrato is your strong suit, select pieces that highlight it. If you are proficient in multiple languages, use that to your advantage. Utilize the Pre-Screen to showcase your best strengths!

4.   Make a list of the repertoire, and stick to it! It is crucial for the success of your Pre-Screen recording experience to become familiar with the repertoire. If you work on one piece for a week and then decide to change it the following week, you will lose one full week, and probably two, until you define the new piece. That's why this planning process is so important. Once you select your pieces, you need to commit to them and become very comfortable with them. Choose wisely!

> *As a buyer of this book, you have access to the RepertoireMatrix™: A specially designed table for performing artists that clarifies the pieces you need to record, their technical and musical challenges, and how to approach them. And a list of common Pre-Screen pieces you can use for your materials. Check out more information about it on the Appendix 1.*

PRO TIP 6: Orchestra Excerpts / Opera or Musical Theater Scenes

If you are applying for a position in an orchestra, opera, or musical theater company, this is almost always a mandatory element they request. Similarly, if you are applying for a university program with a strong emphasis on orchestra, opera, and/or musical theater, having this in your pocket and including it in your Pre-Screen materials (in the "add something else" section) can provide you with an extra profile fit bonus to help you get into the program.

PRO TIP 7: Always take the time to review the full score for everything!

Understanding your role within the larger ensemble, even if you are the soloist, is vital! Whether you're playing the main melodic line, collaborating with other instruments, or accompanying other sections, there is always a carefully crafted musical discourse created by the composer and you MUST understand it. If you need to learn about how this works, I wrote a review of an article that could be a good start. You can access it for free by scanning this QR Code.

A little history for context to understand why it is VERY IMPORTANT:

Back in 2021, when I was working as the Conductor of the Indiana University Opera and Ballet Theater and the Indiana University Symphonies (while pursuing my Doctorate there), I had the privilege of working with four of the best concertmasters in the world (Royal Concertgebouw Orchestra, Dallas Symphony Orchestra, Indianapolis Symphony Orchestra, Minnesota Orchestra, Florida Orchestra, and associate concertmasters of The Cleveland Orchestra, and San Francisco Symphony). Because of my background and experience, I was invited to conduct the orchestras while they were engaged in their orchestra repertoire classes. For more info scan this QR Code.

Something that struck me as very interesting was this: As you know, I was also a violist. I worked as Principal Viola in many professional orchestras, and during my undergraduate studies in viola, I had to take the Orchestra Repertoire class, where I learned and played all the audition excerpts and other orchestral repertoire for viola. During those times, my

professors always emphasized something that now, these prestigious concertmasters echoed to their students while I was conducting, almost in the same words but now in English with various accents: "**A musician MUST ALWAYS know what's happening in the entire orchestra, not just his/her/their specific part.**"

This applies to students as well as professionals.

¡Yes! We (conductors, juries, or other musicians listening to your auditions and pre-screen materials) can tell if you know the score and understand your role within the full orchestral palette at that specific moment in the music, or if you are just playing your part. Therefore, after all the work you did preparing your part, take the time to review the score and understand your role; it will be a huge improvement! If you need help with that, look on my website, and you will see some resources on how to do this effectively.

PRO TIP 8: Consider Using Concert Footage

While recording a session specifically for pre-screen purposes can be beneficial because it reflects your most advanced level and allows you to polish your performance, sometimes actual concert recordings capture a different, more authentic energy for two reasons:

1.   **Live Performance Magic:** When performing in front of an audience, you tap into a different level of artistry that can translate powerfully on camera. You're not just playing for a jury; you're playing for an audience, and the energy exchange can bring out the best in your performance.

2.   **Audience Interaction:** The presence of an audience can provide that final spark of passion or focus that elevates your performance to another level. If possible, include live recordings in your submission, as long as the audio and video quality meet the necessary standards.

Therefore, whenever you define the repertoire you need to prepare, before studying something new and entering this complex process, review whether you already have something of sufficient quality that meets the pre-screen requirements. This could be a great time-saving tool and can enhance your profile as an active artist.

Organizing a Preparation Calendar

Once you've chosen your repertoire, it's time to organize your preparation. This begins with creating a structured practice calendar that allows you to systematically tackle each piece, both technically and musically.

There are many ways to develop this calendar, but the method that has always worked for me having won numerous scholarships at prestigious institutions worldwide, been invited to many top-level international competitions, and secured several professional auditions, is as follows. By the way, research also supports that this is the best way to develop working calendars for the performing arts (more info in my Doctoral Dissertation). Therefore, this method has not only been personally successful for me many times but is also scientifically proven.

This process starts with defining 3 main deadlines:

- **Deadline for sending materials:** It is always good to leave at least one week for emergencies. Sometimes, it's not even you; the programs or systems can have problems. So, be sure to account for that!

- **Deadline for edits:** Since you also have to handle other administrative and logistical processes for the application, you should have your edits ready two weeks in advance. Editing usually takes anywhere from three days to two weeks, depending on the amount of repertoire and your familiarity with editing software (more info in Chapter 4).

- **Deadline for recording:** Since recording is a process that should be done at a good and unhurried pace, it is advisable to allow at least a full week for it.

With all of that in mind, a good preparation period for Pre-Screen materials is typically around 3 months prior to that last deadline for Pre-Screen materials submission. Now, if you don't have all of this time and still want to apply, you have four options:

1.   **Contact the program:** Let them know you just discovered their program, but you're very interested, and ask if they can offer an extension. Depending on their internal deadlines, they might be able to accommodate you.

PRO TIP 9: Talk with director level people

Only the directors of the programs or the main leaders of the organizations have the authority to allow these kinds of changes. If you call and speak with the desk secretary, the most they can do is refer you to the official deadlines and tell you that it is not possible. Try to reach out to directors and/or leaders with a brief personal email explaining why you need an urgent extension. Even better, consider calling them or meeting them in person. This is a case-by-case situation, so it's important to have a compelling reason for your request. Additionally, you need to possess strong interpersonal skills; otherwise, you may not succeed in obtaining an extension.

2.   **Adjust the calendar**: If you're an expert in your major (instrument, voice, or role), try to modify the following calendar and steps to fit your needs. If you're a professional, it will be challenging, but you can do it. It's not ideal to rush, but if you've worked on your major for several years and have already succeeded in other Pre-Screen auditions, it's possible.

3.   **Evaluate your readiness**: If you're at a pre-university or undergraduate level, consider whether it's best to wait until next year. Be honest with yourself. Rushing might create unnecessary stress, and the outcome might not be worth it, possibly even affecting your physical well-being. Assess your level, the repertoire requirements, and what you already have prepared. Seek advice from your professor, a trusted musician friend, or an experienced musician who can offer you an honest opinion.

4.   **Get professional help immediately**: If, after reviewing everything, you decide to go for it, get professional guidance as soon as possible! A professional can create a tailored preparation calendar for you and adjust it as needed, based on your development. This person can focus on the learning and coaching process and planning, allowing you to concentrate fully on your studies. Given the limited

time, every second matters, and you'll need assistance not only with preparation but also with recording and other crucial elements where having an experienced coach makes the difference.

Story time to show you that even in emergencies you still can do it!
Do not give up too soon!

Not many people know how I got my first professional position as a musician. I was only 18 and still working on my first bachelor's degree in viola. I had just started taking conducting as an elective with a clear goal of becoming a conductor. But as you know, to become a conductor, you must have at least a bachelor's degree in another major to ensure you're a great musician before you start moving your hands without a deep understanding of the art. At the time, I was principal viola of various university and youth orchestras but had never played in a professional orchestra or been paid for it. One evening, after my usual 8-9 hours of viola practice, I was about to enjoy a well-deserved milkshake when I got a call from my friend Oscar. He asked, "Diego, do you want to work as a violist in a professional orchestra? Audition tomorrow morning at 10 a.m. downtown. The repertoire is the full Nutcracker, and there are only two viola spots. Are you in?"

At first, I was in shock. The full Nutcracker? Tomorrow? How would I even get the parts to study, let alone prepare for an audition overnight? It was the pre-iPad era, and getting *the music, printing it, and studying it at an audition level felt like an impossible task. After a brief moment of panic, I pulled myself together and said, "Let's do this!" The first hurdle was getting the parts, which either Oscar sent me as a PDF, or I rushed to the university library to get a copy. By 7 p.m., I had the music, but I was exhausted from a full day of practice, and I knew I had to sleep. Auditioning without sleep would have destroyed both my repertoire and technique. So, I had to plan carefully.*

Fortunately, I was in a fantastic bachelor's program that required an orchestra repertoire class, where we learned how to approach the specific demands of being an orchestra player. This training was crucial. It taught me how to study quickly, analyze scores, and prepare efficiently. That night, I had only two hours to study, so I spent the first half-hour planning. I identified which sections I could sight-read confidently, highlighted key viola solos, and pinpointed tricky spots that might be asked in the audition. The next hour and a half was spent practicing slowly the selected spots, focusing on technique, solving bowings, and making sure I was mentally prepared to tackle these passages the next day.

The following morning, during my warm-up, I concentrated on the techniques needed for the specific passages I had studied. I spent two hours polishing the music before heading to the audition venue, which took an hour and a half by bus. During the ride, I also used the time to review the Nutcracker score, ensuring I was prepared to "sight-read" any section as though it were a second look. At the audition, I was lucky.

We rehearsed half the show with the full orchestra before the actual audition, which allowed for more "sight-reading" practice. When it came time to audition, they asked for four or five passages, three of which I had anticipated, and one or two were from the "sight-reading basket." Everything had been meticulously planned, and I won the spot—along with Oscar!

And... that's how I landed my first professional job, playing the Nutcracker and later performing in other operas, concerts, and zarzuelas with the FOSBO (Fundación Orquesta Sinfónica de Bogotá) and also become principal viola in some productions. I stayed for about a year and a half before my conducting studies became too demanding. This experience taught me the importance of always being prepared as a performer.

What seemed like a unique, last-minute opportunity became the norm throughout my career. I've been called to record pre-screenings in less than five hours, conduct orchestras with less than four hours of preparation, and even rehearse and conduct a full opera on short notice. One memorable instance was when I was Assistant and Cover Conductor at IU Opera and Ballet Theater while I was doing my Doctor degree there. One evening, my mentor, Arthur Fagen (distinguished conductor that has lead all the major Opera houses around the globe - Vienna, Metropolitan Opera, Frankfurt, etc) had a personal emergency and had to travel, and he asked me to step in. "Diego, we don't have a conductor for tomorrow. Here's the score. See you at 4 p.m." With less than 18 hours to prepare, I had to learn an entire opera and lead professional performers that were used to working with this outstanding level of conductor. And yes, I did it! I am sure my mentor knew I was ready, and of course every professional performing was very kind (at this very high level usually every one is kind), but also, at a professional level, everything has to be simply: perfect!

Every successful performer I know has been in similar situations, where opportunities arise at the last minute. The only ones who make it are those who are ready. That's why I wanted to share this story, not just for fun, but for three important reasons:

1. *First, in our field, emergencies happen more often than you think, and you must be able to perform or record auditions under pressure. Therefore, if your Pre-Scree has a deadline of less than 3 months, ok great! Used it to also train this ability*

2. *Second, you need a strong mindset and the ability to trust yourself no matter what. Always take your mental health seriously. This is VERY IMPORTANT for performers. Only those who are well-centered and grounded can truly handle the immense pressure that comes with this career.*

3. *Finally, preparation is key. I was able to pull off these last-minute performances because I had the skill and training to back me up.*

That's why I created a unique Auditions and Competitions Training Program at my Private Studio. It's designed to help musicians handle pressure and succeed in any audition, regardless of their major. The program includes coaching on the application process, repertoire building, study scheduling, pre-screen feedback, sight-reading strategies, and body and mind preparation. It even includes four mock auditions or competitions, with feedback from a doctoral-level jury. If you want to be ready for the challenges of our field, check it out on my Private Studio website. Access it by Scaning this QR Code.

And if you ever find yourself in an emergency last-minute situation, don't hesitate to reach out. I sometimes coach and help people navigate those moments when they feel lost and need guidance.

Now, based on this ideal 3 months healthy period of preparation, create a calendar that goes something similar than the following table:

Month	Week	Goal of the week
3rd Month	4	Deadline for applying
	3	Deadline for Editing
	2	RECORDING WEEK
	1	Full runthrough of the full Pieces and/or Excerpts (Non-Stop) based on requirements of each Pre-Screen. Working on details only after.
2nd Month	4	Full runthrough of the Pieces and/or Excerpts (Stopping briefly only after each movement or excerpt is done) based on requirements. Working on details only after the Full runthrough.
	3	Runthrough of each Piece and/or Excerpt. Stopping after the full piece or excerpt to work carefully

		in each of its needs.
	2	RWorking on each Piece and/or Excerpt. Stopping as necessary to work carefully in each of its needs.
	1	Working on each Piece and/or Excerpt. Stopping as necessary to work carefully in each of its needs.
1st Month	4	Working on each Piece and/or Excerpt. Stopping as necessary to work carefully in each of its needs.
	3	Polishing of the Technique required for each Piece and/or Excerpt. Review the excerpts at tempo.
	2	Building of the Technique required for each Piece and/or Excerpt. Review the excerpts at slower tempo
	1	Building of the Technique required for each Piece and/or

		Excerpt. Review the excerpts at slower tempo

PRO TIP 10: Continue with your normal study calendar!

For beginners and mid-level musicians: Remember that this is only a Pre-Screen calendar of goals; it is not a practice calendar. You must continue working on your study activities to achieve these goals. These activities are very personalized, so the best way to define them is by working with your mentor or a person with the necessary experience to guide you.

PRO TIP 11: Work on a different repertoire every day.

If you have a lot of repertoire, follow the "gym workout" strategy. Do not practice all the excerpts every day; this can be very demanding and will create fatigue with the last pieces you study each day. Instead, distribute them throughout the week. For example, practice pieces or excerpts 1, 2, and 3 on day 1; 4, 5, and 6 on day 2; 7, 8, and 9 on day 3; and repeat 1, 2, and 3 on day 4, and so on. There are many ways to define the pairing of pieces, but this will depend on your specific needs, level, and repertoire. If you need help with that, your mentor, professor, or a specialized coach is the best option.

PRO TIP 12: Adjust Calendar as needed!

Your level and each piece will also affect the calendar. As you can see, this is a general calendar of goals. However, remember that each piece will require very specific artistic, musical, and technical development that needs to be carefully integrated into the calendar. If you don't know how to do it, asking your mentor, professor or a specialized coach is the best option.

Okay, this was a long chapter, but it was important because it has laid the foundation for preparing your repertoire. In the next chapters, we'll delve into the recording process itself, covering everything from video setup to audio quality.

> *Remember, as a buyer of this book, you have access to the RepertoireMatrix™: A specially designed table for performing artists that clarifies the pieces you need to record, their technical and musical challenges, and how to approach them. And a list of common Pre-Screen pieces you can use for your materials. Check out more information about it on the Appendix 1.*

Chapter 2: Recording Preparation

The following chapters will be less demanding, as the planning stage has addressed many of the difficulties. Now, we will focus on the more logistical aspects, starting with:

Place

Choosing the right location for your recording is key to ensuring a professional result. For this, remember to review these elements:

- **Quiet Hours:** Make sure the space you select is either soundproof or that you can record during times when there will be minimal external noise. Nothing is more frustrating than nailing a performance, only to have the recording ruined by background noise such as traffic, neighbors, or unexpected interruptions.

- **Clean the Frame:** Just as audio is important, the visual aspect of your recording matters too. Avoid any "visual noise" in your frame. A plain background, such as a theater or a simple white wall, is ideal. If you don't have access to such a space, ensure that your environment is tidy and free of distractions. Remember, the aesthetic of your video will reflect your professionalism and attention to detail.

- **Good Lighting**: Your lighting setup should allow the jury to clearly see your facial expressions, hand movements, and full-body technique. Natural light is great if available, but if not, try to use a few light sources from different angles to ensure there are no harsh shadows or overly dark spots in your frame.

Recording Equipment

Recording quality will depend heavily on the equipment you use. However, with creativity, you can achieve great results even without professional gear.

- **Camera Quality:** Nowadays, many smartphones offer high-quality video capabilities, often supporting 1080p or even 4K resolution. If you have access to a DSLR or professional camera, that's even better. But if not, a modern phone should suffice for a pre-screen video, as long as it captures clear images and movements.

- **Framing:** Pay careful attention to the framing of your video. Some programs may have specific requirements, so be sure to follow them exactly to avoid disqualification. If no requirements are listed, follow these general guidelines:

- Include your entire body and instrument (for string players, this includes the bow).
- Leave a bit of extra room around you to allow for movement and prevent any part of you or your instrument from being cut off.
- If performing with a pianist, ensure that both you and the pianist are clearly visible.
- For conductors, ensure the camera captures your full movements, as well as the first stands of the orchestra. If performing with an ensemble, it's important to show a comprehensive view. You can see examples of good frames for conductors by scanning this QR Code.

- **Microphone:** While phone cameras can provide decent video, their built-in microphones are often inadequate for professional-quality recordings. To improve audio, try using an external microphone positioned around 3-4 meters (10-13 feet) from you.

- **Sound Check:** Always perform a sound check before you start recording. Play a short excerpt, listen back, and adjust the microphone's distance to ensure clarity and balance between your instrument or voice and the surrounding acoustics. Avoid capturing mechanical sounds (e.g., bow against strings or keys on the piano) if the microphone is too close, or creating an echo if it's too far. In certain contexts (such as Baroque or vocal music), a small amount of echo may be beneficial, so it's worth experimenting and adjusting depending on the repertoire.

- **Concert Recordings:** If you're using audio from a live concert, make sure it's recorded from a spot that best captures the sound. The venue's sound engineer, the assistant conductor, or a friend with trusted ears can often provide guidance on where to place microphones for optimal sound.

Outfit

Your appearance plays an important role in how you present yourself as an artist. Your outfit should reflect the artistic role you're applying for. Whether it's for a professional role or a university program, you are already an artist, and your attire should demonstrate your commitment to the performance. Think about what you would wear to an in-person audition and replicate that for your pre-screen recording.

Choose an outfit that is both sophisticated and comfortable. The best concert attire not only looks professional but also allows you to perform without distraction.

PRO TIP 13: Practice in Your Outfit:

Make sure to practice in your chosen outfit to avoid any surprises on recording day. You want to be familiar with how it feels so that you can focus entirely on your performance.

PRO TIP 14: Practice in Your Shoes:

Practicing in your shoes is particularly important, especially if you're wearing high heels or new, formal footwear. If your recording session will last two hours, make sure you're comfortable standing or moving in them for at least that long, so discomfort doesn't interfere with your performance.

Planning Your Takes

When planning your recording, decide whether you will complete everything in one session or spread it across multiple days.

- **Back-to-Back or Separate Days?** Consider whether it's feasible to complete your recording in a single session or if it would be better to spread the process over multiple days. This depends on your stamina, the complexity of the repertoire, and the availability of your recording space.

- **Organize the order of your recording session:** If the university or organization is not requiring you to record everything in one take, the order in which you record doesn't matter. Editing can take care of that later. Therefore, organize your repertoire in a way that is comfortable for you. The best approach will depend on the specific repertoire, the time of day you're recording, your study habits, and your strengths and weaknesses. It's helpful to get advice from a coach who knows you well and can plan the session in a way that facilitates a smoother recording process.

PRO TIP 15: Practice the Takes:

As discussed in the previous chapter, rehearse the entire recording process during the final week, including any activity you need between takes, so you're prepared for potential challenges. The more comfortable you are with the setup, the smoother the actual recording will be.

By preparing your setting, equipment, and planning ahead, you'll ensure your recording session goes smoothly and that your pre-screen video is as professional and polished as possible. In the next chapter, we'll explore specific strategies to help you manage the recording day itself and how to approach multiple takes.

Chapter 3: Recording

Practicing the Takes

Just like any performance, rehearsing your recordings is crucial to ensure you're fully prepared for the actual session.

- **Do Trial Runs with Equipment:** Practice some takes with your equipment to get used to the camera's presence and adjust any awkward movements or habits that might appear on screen. The goal is to become so familiar with the process that you almost forget you're being recorded, allowing your artistry to come through naturally.

- **Camera Awareness:** Learn to move comfortably within the frame and project your performance, whether it's with your instrument, voice, or conducting. Be mindful of how you appear on camera — posture, movements, and facial expressions all matter.

Be Prepare for Multiple Takes

Recording can be an exhausting process, both mentally and physically, but it's important to plan for multiple takes. One of the keys to a successful recording is giving yourself enough time and space to get the best results possible.

- **Pace Yourself:** Don't expect perfection on the first try. Mentally prepare for multiple takes so that each performance becomes more relaxed, authentic, and focused. Often, the first few takes help warm you up and get comfortable in front of the camera. By the time you've done several takes, you'll feel more natural, and the stress of recording will fade away.

- **Ample Memory and Battery:** Before you begin, ensure your camera or phone and microphone settings have enough memory and a fully charged battery to handle as many takes as necessary. The last thing you want is to run out of space mid-session or scramble to recharge during a creative flow.

- **Eat Properly and Stay Hydrated:** This may sound basic, but with the stress of recording, it's easy to forget to eat properly and stay hydrated. Not eating well or staying hydrated will negatively affect the quality of your recordings.

PRO TIP 16: Eat Before!

Eat before recording as if you're about to do a full, two-hour, demanding workout. You shouldn't be too full, but you need enough energy for a long, challenging activity.

PRO TIP 17: Water!

Always have a bottle of water with you, and after each full take, drink a little. It will help calm you down and make the experience more enjoyable.

Involving Friends or Family?

Depending on your personality, having a few familiar faces around can help relieve some of the tension of recording and provide a small live audience.

- **Supportive Presence:** Ask a close friend or family member to be present during your recording. Their support can help you feel more at ease and simulate a live performance environment.

- **Get Feedback:** Having others there can also be beneficial for getting immediate feedback on aspects like posture, framing, and energy. They may notice things that you might overlook and can help you improve in real-time.

But remember, everyone is different; some people may feel more overwhelmed when there are others in the room. Know yourself and choose what works best for you!

Plan for Extra Takes

Once you've completed your initial takes, don't hesitate to review the footage and assess what works and what could be improved.

- **Immediate Review:** After recording a few takes, take short breaks to review what you've captured. This gives you the opportunity to spot technical issues (e.g., framing, audio balance, lighting) or performance aspects you might want to refine.

PRO TIP 18: Don't Rush and enjoy!:

Set aside enough time in your schedule to plan for extra takes if necessary. Sometimes, it's after several recordings that you reach the performance that feels right. Be patient with yourself and allow for this flexibility. Remember, even professionals, like the London Philharmonic or LA Repertoire Orchestras, are accustomed to having two full days of recording sessions in the studio for only one symphony or movie track. Quality takes time, enjoy the process!

In summary, the key to a successful recording session is to stay patient, focused, and open to multiple takes. The more relaxed and prepared you are, the better your final product will be. In the next chapter, we'll explore the post-production process, including reviewing and editing your recordings to ensure they are polished and professional.

Chapter 4: Editing

Knowing Your Audience and Their Requirements

Before diving into editing, it's crucial to revisit the guidelines and specifications provided by the program, organization, or competition you're applying to. Yes, one more time, amid the excitement of preparation, it's easy to overlook specific details, so it's worth reviewing them again. Also, at this moment it's important to focus on understanding who will be watching your video and how to best portray yourself.

- **Check the Requirements:** Some auditions may request a full, unedited take, while others might allow you to piece together segments from multiple takes. Be sure to follow the rules exactly. Submitting an edited video when a full take is required could lead to disqualification.

- **Understand the Audience:** If your video is meant for an audience of professional musicians or experienced artists, avoid unnecessary cuts or edits, especially within the same piece. These viewers will want to assess your raw talent, consistency, and musical expression, so an unaltered performance may work in your favor.

"Cutting" the video

When editing a pre-screen video recording, it's important to leave two or three seconds of silence before and after the music starts. This creates a professional impression and mimics the experience of a live audition. Unless it's a concert recording with short excerpts, this brief silence frames the performance effectively, allowing the juries to feel as though they are watching a live take. Just ensure the pause is kept short and the video feels authentic and in-the-moment.

Avoid Editing within the Same Piece!

While it's common for professional recordings to include cuts from multiple concerts to create a "perfect" version (many "live" recordings that are highly publicized for sale are actually made up of several live takes combined into one seamless performance), auditions are different. Judges want to see your performance as close to a live experience as possible.

- **One Piece, One Take**: For individual pieces, avoid making cuts within the same piece. Consistency is key. Auditions are about showcasing both your technical ability and artistic flow, and editing out mistakes may give the impression that you're hiding weaknesses.

-   **No speed or audio editing:** While some noise reduction and sound balancing might be helpful, it's best to avoid any significant audio correction for Pre-Screen materials. Yes, it's important to produce a strong, professional pre-screen recording, and light audio editing may seem tempting. However, keep in mind that the purpose of a pre-screen is for the jury to assess your sound and current level (both strengths and weaknesses), and an overly edited video can lead to disqualification, as it may present a misleading portrayal of your abilities.

Story time for context and relaxation:

As impressed as I would be with myself if I could create the next "story" from nothing to explain an important point, I must sadly admit that the following is a real-life event that was a well-known story in Colombia. I am trying to portray it as a short tale using my artistic liberty to avoid names and specifics since I was not one of the jurors present and I listen to the story by the voices of others. And also, because despite my total rejection of this kind of practice, the person involved has already faced many hardships. Therefore, the purpose of this is not to breathe down anyone's neck; it is simply to explain a point.

From Local Short-Term "Star" to National Long-Lasting Fake:
When Pre-Screen Goes Out of Control

In the vibrant world of classical music, where passion meets precision, there was a young pianist whose ambition outshone his preparation. He had set his sights on a prestigious piano competition that promised to catapult the winner into the spotlight, offering opportunities that most musicians only dream of. However, rather than dedicating himself to the rigorous practice required to master the challenging repertoire, and the pre-screen recording, he devised a shortcut that he thought might secure his success: he submitted a pre-screen audio recording of a renowned pianist's performance. After all, the competition only required audio, and with so many recordings to review, who would notice?

To his astonishment, the gamble paid off. He was accepted into the competition. It felt like a stroke of luck, a golden ticket to a world he longed to be a part of. But as he prepared to take the stage, a gnawing sense of unease lingered in the back of his mind. When the moment finally arrived, he sat at the grand piano, heart racing, and began to play. It quickly became apparent to the jury and the audience that he was far from the level of the famed pianist whose recording he had submitted. Gasps of surprise rippled through the hall as he stumbled through the piece, and, unable to maintain the facade, the judges stopped him mid-performance and disqualified him.

But the repercussions didn't end there. The jurors, alarmed by the stark contrast between his recorded submission and his actual playing, delved deeper into the application materials. It wasn't long before they uncovered the truth: the audio submission was indeed a famous pianist's work. In a move that reverberated throughout the music community, the jury issued a press release outlining the incident, naming the "pianist" and urging the industry to steer clear of this fraud. The young man's reputation was shattered, and what could have been the beginning of a promising career instead became a cautionary tale.

The moral of this story is clear: shortcuts in pre-screen applications are fraught with risk. It is far better to be honest about one's abilities and continue to work hard than to present a façade that can only lead to disgrace. The young pianist's decision to cut corners not only cost him an opportunity but ultimately damaged his career irreparably. In the realm of music, authenticity and integrity are paramount; the journey may be challenging, but the rewards of genuine growth and development far outweigh the fleeting allure of quick success.

This incident also highlighted the inherent problems of relying solely on audio recordings in pre-screening processes. While the absence of visuals may seem convenient, it opens the door to potential deceit and misrepresentation. As polemic as it could sound, in a field where artistry is often absorbed by all senses, including the eyes as much as the ears, the lack of visual context can lead to misinterpretations and unfair advantages. Or fraud as we can see in the previous "story"

But this is a conversation for another time, one that I have explored extensively in my doctoral dissertation. I've also distilled these complex ideas into a more digestible format aimed at artistic administrators, who play a crucial role in crafting fair protocols for auditions and competitions. It's their responsibility to ensure that the processes in place safeguard against the very pitfalls that led to our piano protagonist's downfall. But if you are curious, you can see that in my Doctoral Dissertation, or in the publications by the Performing Arts Laboratory - Press.

In the end, this story serves not only as a cautionary tale for aspiring musicians but also as a reminder of the ongoing dialogue about fairness and transparency in the performing arts.

Investing in Video Editing

The quality of your video matters. Even if the audition committee doesn't explicitly state that video quality is a factor, it can subconsciously influence how they perceive your work.

- **Why Quality Matters:** When audition judges are reviewing hundreds of applications, a poorly edited or low-quality video may not be taken as seriously as a polished one. You've already invested time and effort in preparing and recording—don't lose points over avoidable technical issues.

- **As much as possible, use Professional Tools:** I personally recommend Adobe Premiere Pro. While it might not be as user-friendly as you'd like, it's a highly capable tool for video editing, and for a pre-screen video, you won't need extensive editing. There are countless tutorial videos on YouTube that can guide you through any feature or effect you want to apply. However, if you have financial restrictions, there is always the possibility of looking for free software alternatives online. Just make sure to allocate enough extra time to ensure it looks as good as possible.

On the other hand, if you're unsure or short on time, consider hiring a professional editor to ensure your video looks its best. For extra support, the Performing Arts Laboratory offers branding and marketing development services, including help with video editing. It's worth checking out if you're not confident in your editing skills or you are pressed for time. You can review them by scanning this QR Code.

Organizing the Video for Maximum Impact

The order in which you present your pieces can shape the audience's impression of you.

• **First Impressions Matter:** Together with your CV, Pre-Screen material serves as your introduction to the judges, so you want to grab their attention in the right way. If there are specific requirements regarding the order of the pieces or excerpts, be sure to follow them, they are there for a reason. If there are no specific guidelines, start with your strongest performance. A friend or trusted professional can often help you determine which piece that is.

PRO TIP 19: Consider Flow:

After your best piece, plan the rest of the video strategically. Keep the energy and momentum consistent so that your final performance leaves a lasting impression.

In summary, the editing process is your final opportunity to ensure your hard work is presented in the best possible light. Pay attention to the details, ensure your video is polished and professional, and consider how your submission reflects your personal brand as an artist. Following these steps will help ensure that your audition video stands out from the competition.

Adding Essential Information

Your video must clearly present all the necessary details about your performance. Failing to provide this information can be a costly oversight.
Include the following:

- Title of the work
- Full name of the composer
- Date and place of the recording
- Names of any additional performers (if it's a group performance)

Make sure all required elements are neatly displayed and easy to read, preferably at the start of the video.

Some programs may also ask for this information as subtitles during the video or at a specific section in the uploading platform, so have it easily accessible.

Adding and Maintaining Your Personal Brand

Every video you submit is not just an audition but also an opportunity to build your personal brand as an artist (no matter your level). Your brand should reflect professionalism and artistic quality.

- **Why Branding Matters:** The music world is highly competitive, and over time, you want your name and image to be associated with high-quality performances. Even at the start of your career, it's important to begin shaping your professional image.

- **How to Add Your Brand:** Include your name and any personal branding elements (like a logo) in the video, ensuring they are presented professionally and consistently. A well-placed, well-designed watermark can also enhance the polish of your video and help viewers remember you.

    Do this professionally and with elegance. This isn't a marketing video! There is a delicate balance between being perceived as professional and being over-branded. If you are unsecure what that means, as I told you before, the Performing Arts Laboratory offers branding services that can guide you through effective branding strategies.

Chapter 5: Final Tips

Before uploading, get a Second Opinion

Before uploading your video, always get feedback from at least two people:

- **An Expert:** Preferably your current professor or the coach who helped you prepare the repertoire. Their perspective is invaluable, as they understand the artistic and technical standards required for success.

- **A Music Trusted Individual:** This could be someone whose opinion you value in the music community, as they can provide an overall sense of how the video comes across from a fresher perspective. Since you have been working with your professor or coach, they may be somewhat accustomed to your style. Fresh opinions are always valuable because they bring a different perspective. Sometimes, small details you might overlook can make a significant difference.

Having multiple perspectives ensures that your work meets the highest standards before submission. If you don't have the people to help you, and you need any help with that... either me, or the Performing Arts Laboratory can be that extra opinion you need. You can contact us on our websites.

Saving your recordings

- **YouTube Upload:** Adobe Premiere Pro has an option to export in high quality that works perfectly with YouTube. Always choose HD for the best visual and audio clarity. The extra time it takes to process in HD is completely worth it, as it demonstrates to the juries that you understand that quality is the essence of music and art.

- **Be Thorough with Details:** Ensure that your video link works flawlessly and that judges can access it easily. With hundreds of applications, technical mistakes are often reasons for disqualification, please don't be that person!

- **Avoid Private Links:** Never share the video using privacy settings like "Private" or "Only you can view." If you are using password protection, make sure to send the password alongside the video link. Nothing frustrates judges more than having to chase down technical issues. If they are in a good mood, they may email you to request the password again. However, unless there aren't many applicants, it is very unusual for them to revisit missing videos, as time is money, and this applies to the performing arts as well, since juries are usually very busy professionals.

PRO TIP 20: ALWAYS GO FOR HIGH-QUALITY!

Remember that with your materials, you aren't just presenting your ability to play the instrument; you are showcasing your professionalism. High-quality sound and visuals enhance your overall presentation.

PRO TIP 21: Use great quality recordings to start creating your brand.

Using high-quality recordings is essential for building your unique brand as an artist, even if you're just starting. If you have a well-recorded video that trusted and experienced professionals agree is strong, don't hesitate to publish and share it. You own the rights to your performance, and you never know who might see your video and offer you an audition or even a concert opportunity. However, before you share your recording outside of audition settings for marketing purposes, it's important to double-check copyright details to ensure you have all the necessary permissions.

While you hold the rights to your performance, some music may still be under copyright, meaning that you might need authorization from the composer or rights holders before publishing your video. Although the majority of pieces requested for pre-screen recordings are in the public domain, it's still worth verifying to avoid any legal issues. If you need help navigating these rights or marketing your recording, the Performing Arts Laboratory offers services specifically designed to assist artists with branding and marketing development. It's worth exploring for professional guidance in this area.

Keeping a Local Copy for Other Platforms

Some organizations or universities use specific platforms, such as GetAccepted or other internal submission systems. It's important to have your videos saved on your PC in a high-quality format so you can easily re-upload them when necessary. Your video may need to be submitted to multiple institutions or organizations, so having it ready in different formats is essential for efficient application management.

Backing-Up Your Recordings for Future Use

Once your video is uploaded, shared, etc., don't stop there. Save all of your recordings for the future. Invest in a good external hard drive to store not only this audition but also future concerts, rehearsals, master classes, chamber music performances, and other significant recordings. You never know when these might come in handy. I regret not keeping all my recordings from past projects, especially those of me playing viola. And also other conducting videos I lost because of a bad quality external drive. Looking back, these materials could have been incredibly useful for new opportunities or even just as milestones in my artistic journey. Don't make the same mistake, archive your hard work!

Acknowledging and Sharing Your Accomplishments

Take a moment to **congratulate yourself** on the immense effort you've put into this process. Recording are labor-intensive, but you've done it. Whether or not you land the spot, this is a significant achievement that will help you grow as a professional musician. Share your journey with friends and fellow artists. This Pre-Screen recording was a major stepping stone in your career, showcasing your growth as an artist. Sharing photos from the process, or short clips of your Pre-Screen material can not only be rewarding but also boost your personal brand, regardless of your current level.

And if this guide helped you in any way, don't forget to tag us down: **#MasteringPreScreen** @barbosa_vasquez and @performingartslab

By following these final steps, you'll ensure your pre-screen materials are polished, professional, and ready to make a strong impression on your application and your career as a whole.

Good luck!

Kind regards!
Maestro Diego Barbosa-Vásquez
Opera, Orchestra, and Ballet Conductor & Scholar
Doctor in Music & Expert in Performing Arts Sustainability
www.barbosavasquez.com

Appendix 1

Extra Materials for Pre-Screen Preparation

In collaboration with the Performing Arts Laboratory, the Barbosa-Vásquez Private Studio, and Fundación Intersociedad-E&P, we have created a special space for all stakeholders in the Performing Arts who want to develop a sustainable relationship within the field: the PAL Community. You can access this community by simply registering on the following website. As a buyer of this book, you will receive a **free one-year subscription** (with proof of your book purchase). This subscription provides access to valuable materials specially designed for individuals like you, offering an extra boost and expert support in preparing and recording your pre-screen materials.

Since the Performing Arts are constantly evolving, the materials and exclusive resources in the PAL Community are regularly updated to ensure everyone has access to the most advanced and up-to-date information. From the time of this book's publication until your access begins, you may find additional resources available. For now, as a buyer of this book and a contributor to the mission of developing a better and more sustainable Performing Arts field, you will have exclusive access to:

- The RepertoireMatrix™: A specially designed table for performing artists that clarifies the pieces you need to record, their technical, musical and artistic challenges, and how to approach them.

- A List of Common Pre-Screen or Audition Pieces: This serves as a helpful guide if you're unsure about which materials to record.

- Personal/Artistic Statement Video Script: A basic script to guide you through creating this often-challenging video, which is increasingly required by schools, competitions, and organizations.

To access these resources, just scan this QR Code

or visit:

www.performingartslab.com/prescreen